EON

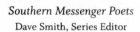

Southern Messenger Poets
Dave Smith, Series Editor

EON

POEMS

T. R. HUMMER

Louisiana State University Press)|(*Baton Rouge*

Published by Louisiana State University Press
Copyright © 2018 by T. R. Hummer
All rights reserved
Manufactured in the United States of America
LSU Press Paperback Original
First printing

Designer: Michelle A. Neustrom
Typefaces: Whitman, text; Penumbra MM, display

Some of these poems have been previously published, as follows: *Ascent:* "Modus Operandi"; *Cutthroat:* "A street corner"; *Literati Quarterly:* "Cold Case: Easter, 2014," "Freudian Sleep," "Legendary Head"; *Mantis:* "Earthworks," "Forensics," "Greek Fire," "Water Trial"; *Plume:* "Eugenics," "Passing"; *White Stag:* "A Diagram of Emotions That Have No Name in the Mother Tongue," "Genotype," "Profession."

The second section of this book, "Urn," was published as a limited-edition chapbook by Diode Editions.

"Cheap Glass Vase at the Jazz Singer's Grave" was originally published in *The Normal School* and was reprinted in *Five Points* as part of a memorial to Philip Levine.

Library of Congress Cataloging-in-Publication Data

Names: Hummer, T. R., author.
Title: Eon : poems / T.R. Hummer.
Description: Baton Rouge : Louisiana State University Press, [2018] | Series:
   Southern messenger poets
Identifiers: LCCN 2017038113| ISBN 978-0-8071-6779-3 (pbk. : alk. paper) |
   ISBN 978-0-8071-6780-9 (pdf) | ISBN 978-0-8071-6781-6 (epub)
Classification: LCC PS3558.U445 A6 2018 | DDC 811/.54—dc23
LC record available at https://lccn.loc.gov/2017038113

The paper in this book meets the guidelines for permanence and durability of the Committee on Production Guidelines for Book Longevity of the Council on Library Resources. ∞

—For Theo and Victor
and Beth and Emma

If death itself were to die, would it have a ghost, and would the ghost of death visit the dead in the guise of someone alive, if only to fright them from any temptation to return?

—WILLIAM GASS

CONTENTS

II. URN

III. EON

CODA

EON

EARTHWORKS

This is a simple furrow, plowed straight across the plot
Of Black Prairie, a stand of beans, braced by wooden forms
On either side. The boy sits, a brooding brat, in the black dirt
Watching his father hoeing. Tilth. Dead bean leaves. Worms.

He balks. The father sweats; his straw hat darkens with it.
Irish and German, his forebears took steerage,
Peasants, to change their names and squat
On a section of soil, grow beans, beget, and age.

The boy hates dirt. He hates the ammoniac stink
Of broadcast fertilizer. Asked to weed, he refuses.
His father ignores him. Rigorous, he loses
Himself in the plain *ecstasis* of his work.

Ecstasis. Ethos. Gravitas. Words from another world
Where men thrust spear-points through the teeth's barrier,
And children's names are plumes of greasy smoke that curls
From burning cities on hillsides incised with the gods' imprimatur.

His father understands *harrow*, what *singletree* means,
How to keep a dumb mule steady, drawing a sulky-plow.
The boy is that story. Overhead, the sky's plowed row
Is straight and pellucid blue between borders of beans.

—In memoriam Seamus Heaney, 1939–2013

I

MURDER

Looking for the body, we found hundreds of burned-out lightbulbs
in a clearing. Found four bodies, not the body we were looking for.

—MICHAEL MARTONE

Mother, mother! I am killed, mother!

—WILLIAM SHAKESPEARE

SCENE

The woman liked to make love late, after everyone
    was asleep, including the man, whom she would wake
By throwing one leg across him and whispering in their private
    language, which is the code of all lovers, until he returned
From the other world, where his ghosts clung to him;
    she was stronger than all the magnificent dead, and ripped him
Out of his own future, though the spirits moaned in exactly the same
    key she moaned in, being like a landscape: entered.

PREMEDITATED

A shattered plain near sunset: the men in neat formation
    beside their caissons. Someone found them
Scattered after the battle, and, moved by their disorder,
    dragged the corpses into rows for a last inspection.
But even dead, the men go on talking quietly,
    comparing their dishonors, planning their funerals.

WATER TRIAL

Euthanized, the retriever lies dense with attention
    those last moments, then bares his teeth
Delicately, to show he accepts this one final order:
    a life is a vessel of ice hauling a cargo of water
Over a horizonless lake, and when the seams uncaulk
    and the bulkheads buckle, the surfaces disappear—
Prime matter collapsing into itself and through the silver
    meniscus, emptied, overmastered, carrying nothing home.

PROFESSION

Traces of blood in the sunset, smudges and residues.
    It hurts most when we are least mindful, like
St. Sebastian sleepwalking through a skyscape,
    fletching arrows of dispassion, or Maudgalyāyana
Mortaring the stones of his martyrdom into the lintel
    of the next life. Stay awake, the elm mutters
To the woodcutter, its disciple. You'll forget the judgment
    of smoke and ash soon enough. You'll stumble
Over the threshold, distracted by your own axe.

A DIAGRAM OF EMOTIONS THAT HAVE
NO NAME IN THE MOTHER TONGUE

The hunger for the inner bark of a solitary tree
    that grows on an uncharted island at the end
Of a burnt map of the mind. The longing for unshattering.
    Or of the crows circling a beleaguered hawk:
They are burning to avenge a future violence.
    Unspeakable, the spark of synapses in a mind
Not yours. Things happen beyond happening. The snake
    numinous for mouse blood. The brilliance of swarming after God.

FORENSICS

Mineral, exposed in cracked strata
    to wind on a ridge, broken by sunlight;
Chemical, dissolved in promiscuous solvents,
    runneled downslope into an obsidian crevasse;
Skeletal, laid in state with ethereal rowboats and lapdogs,
    surrounded by bodyguards, lacquered and sealed:
Old skull of mine, your destiny is formal. When the music
    starts again, get a haircut. Buy a pistol. Find a job.

GENOTYPE

The old man stands at his kitchen counter
    naked, skinning rabbits. Out the window
A snowy field fluoresces in moonlight. The big knife
    is heavy in his hand. His hand is heavy.
Gravity has made him a cruel marriage, but he survives it
    reading a kabbalah in the snow, which is inscribed
With a chaos of tracks, as though a wrack
    of rabbits had convened to observe an execution,
Lingered to ruminate awhile, and then moved on.

LEGENDARY HEAD

In a hatbox left on a broke-back bench
    in a station of the metro;
In a gym bag abandoned on the courthouse lawn
    at midnight, marked by the dominant X
Of starlight, a little blood leaking from a raveling seam.
    Visionary: as though the ripening eyes
Were infused with napalm and mescaline.
    Somewhere a torso, fragmented, stumbles,
Groping for its pedestal. Museums are choked with bodies.
    They are victims of a life that can never change.
Who was he? We will not know. We do not want to
    see him there, a lost effect, a crime, a severance package.

EUGENICS

An abandoned clinic, empty as if after a war,
    still furnished with chairs of medicinal green,
Desks the color of old photographs, a beveled mirror
    discolored by sunlight, catalyzed with dust.
In the black light of consciousness, smears
    of blood and semen glow on surfaces
No one would have thought contaminated by any
    trace of human leakage. It is the antechamber
Of a mind disordered by the impure chemistry
    of selfhood. Inside the sealed file drawers,
Row after row of folders, each tab inscribed
    in gold, where the priests stood in their apparel
With trumpets, and the Levites, the sons of Asaph,
    with cymbals, to praise all that has gone
To sediment, oxide, and carbonaceous brume.

IN THE PARLOR WITH A PIPE WRENCH

At the moment of impact, the body loses weight
    equivalent to the mass of one meager soul,
But who can tell? A wrench embedded in a skull
    is a heavy thing. And the killer flinches at the sight
Of doilies, china kittens, chintz, and hideous floral carpet.

FREUDIAN SLEEP

Wherein submarines glide among iron nets
    and rusting mines spiked with kelp.
Wherein vicious sexual morays probe the vents.
    I do the dead man's float, predictable, Oedipal.
Full fathom five among coral and whelks,
    my father does it too, a depth charge and a pearl
In the riptide of his subconscious. In the twentieth year
    of his being dead, I drift bloody-handed in the dark
Body of the world, Nazis in my periscope, *Mamá, O ma mer.*

PERSON OF INTEREST

As if he had lived too long in the clearing
    behind the quarry, where his parents
Were still burning stumps of hazard trees their parents
    axed when he was born; as if he had gone on,
Himself, with that ancient labor until the heat
    of the bonfires left scars on the backs of his eyes;
As if the irregular perimeter of the zone he worked
    were all of it, everything, the whole of sacred Being:
So he recognized himself, he marked himself, he took
    the great crosscut to his own roots and bore it down.

PASSING

They lay the old woman in the back seat of a car,
    propped her there with pillows, packed
Necessities in the trunk. They drove through the town
    where she'd lived for ninety years, passing
Banked azaleas, flags, an old bigot walking a dog,
    the church parking lot of smoking slag, a street
Of shacks where children threw stones at a mangy cat.
    They stopped at the clinic, where a nurse came out
With her injection. She would drift to the distant city
    on a riptide of chemistry. *Never to return*
Seemed nothing. *Never again* faded in some oceanic
    false recollection. What mattered now was the journey,
The horizon of unknown, shining buildings, the blaze
    of hecatombs touched off in memory of the great departed,
The painless angels with their so far unmapped cruelties.

COLD CASE: EASTER, 2014

The print is atavistic, spatulate—an arch,
    not a whorl, at its center—of the kind palmists call
The Murderer's Thumb. It graces a stained stone, still
    out of alignment, thrown an eon ago, collecting
A tracery of now near-fossilized skin cells in its grain.
    And here we discover rust-eaten nails, and here
A few rotted threads of linen our forensics reveal
    was soaked in sour wine vinegar. They lie
Beside a circlet of brambly material, rotted almost
    to nothing. History has hidden the motive, but the means
Remain discoverable to one who has a little faith
    in methodology. Yonder is the garden. Here is the hill
Of the skull above a little plain where the witnesses
    scattered. If you listen hard, you can almost hear
The lamentations released by hammering—for hammering
    there surely was. *Too long a sacrifice can make a stone
Of the heart.* And the blood that has spattered this stump
    of a rough-planed beam: was it ever even human?

AUBADE OF INSCAPE

Gerard Manley Hopkins, June 8, 1889

Impatient of penultimates, Father, you are fire-
    glazed, galvanized. The fever has wracked you harder
Than your God. Unless the fever *is* your God.
    It is Ireland; it is morning. Outside, cloud-
clotted, the sky defies close reading, but the harrier
    hawk flies in grandeur there, perfectly defined.
In your Jesuit cell, your Jesuit cells are wearier
    than your muse, who keeps demanding more.
Today is your death day. I should not call you *you*,
    ghost. That summer morning, then, a lover said goodbye
To the world. Bit by a flea from a Jesuit sewer rat,
    he burned with earthly typhoid, annealed, and died.
He had complained the pipes were leaky. He knew
    the fury of the ultimate inscape darkening there, and entered it.

MODUS OPERANDI

The veteran sits like an ancient statue at noon
    under the Ponderosas, white and fragmentary.
His war is lifetimes past. His caretakers roll him and leave him
    in the park. Today they have him surrounded
By small airplanes. What does he not remember
    about dismemberment? Now, one by one he launches them
Into the desert air, leaning forward in the motorized
    wheelchair, looking up toward clouds where they drone
Unmanned, blazing down destruction on hostile firmament.

EVIDENCE ROOM

Moonlight stains the strand, tide out, a colorless
    dinghy left belly up on the pebble beach.
All of this is memory, but not of any specific moment,
    an amalgam of the mind's experience of many worlds
In which a body may appear anywhere, anyone's,
    neck askew, lights out in the corneas,
While over the stone pathway, a luminous residue
    of God's semen attenuates and fades.

PENTOBARBITAL

A sudden blankness, the meditation of a narcoleptic,
    July sky beyond the mast of a schooner becalmed
In horizonless water. Ice age, the biochemistry of onyx.
    They strap the prisoner down, and prepare the needle.
Everything that happens now is colorless, though bitter,
    black dog in a midnight alley, dreaming of carbon.

ALGOR MORTIS

The cable technician labors hours in a tiny attic
    finished with tenpenny nails and fiberglass
To move electrons eons displaced from God's firstborn,
    HE 1523-0901 perhaps, a fireball so old
We cannot give it a true name, but its ancient emanations
    press pictures of canned soup, cats, and politicians' faces
Into minds too tired to care. It is December, and sleet
    statics the tin roof over the worker's head
As he clicks shut the relay box, supercooled in the rafters,
    Invisible to those below as x-rays to a femur,
Creatures in shadowy rooms an infinity beneath him
    rapt in their vision of circumstance and star gas.

OF THE FATHERS

The old man and the boy hiding in the culvert
    are strangers. And yet they cling as if one
Could save the other. The butchered city scatters
    its scraps for hectares toward every horizon,
But this is no apocalypse. This is an ordinary morning
    of the world's ongoingness. And if the boy is screaming
At the angle his forearm makes with the bone
    protruding, it is his misunderstanding
That pains him. He knows nothing of the mundane.
    But the old man is screaming too, and the nameless
Soldiers and their common bayonets are no excuse
    for his indecorousness. He was taught a grown man bows
To necessity only, but when it comes, he bows completely.
    His forefathers worshiped at the altar of the chariot;
He is the acolyte of drones. What are the two of them doing
    half buried here, feeling the earth grow grave
With the weight of ordnance? On another day, this child
    might knife him and liberate his watch. But now
He must steel himself. He must become the blade
    of God. Beyond the moment, the acid on his tongue
And the Humvees' crush, like Abraham he is fated,
    a patriarch. He has a son to teach.

CIRCUMSTANTIAL

If there were wind, the morning would be alive,
    the olive trees would knit their quaint garrote
As it was in the beginning. Even the portal of the stream
    is choked, and the wren's nest, and the otter's den in the berm.
We have to work backward from the fact of the body,
    which is absent. We have to solve for a spotless X.
Someone was here once, a pregnant schoolgirl, a worker
    in the olive grove. Now there is nothing but an unknown
Fugitive, who goes about life as if life were the one mistake.

ERASURE

A cormorant had lifted from the inky estuary and lapsed
  behind the bridge moments ago perhaps, etching
A shape in the water unrelated to its body, incommensurate
  with its hunger, but expressing a luminous turbulence
We could not trace back by any logic to the bird we never saw:
  the way an old man opens a hole in the ground and pulls it
In behind him, and we remember him as *father*, no matter who he was.

CHAIN OF CUSTODY

There was a storm, and after, he found the ancient cedar
    gone down in the barn lot. Since his grandparents' time
It had lifted its pitted spear-tip against the stars,
    but the stars are exacting assassins: the grandparents gone,
The parents gone, and now the tree, and the henhouse
    it fell on. He had built it with his father
One spring, and in the summer he had married,
    the ring passed down from his mother's dead hand.
Over the walls of Babylon, into the ruined valleys of Detroit,
    constellations of vultures revolved. He took his saw
To the great bole and piece by piece considered:
    Planks for a new henhouse. For his wife a jewelry box.
Small toys for the children. Shavings for winter tinder.
    For himself, a fragrant coffin. A stake for his pitted heart.

WITNESS

Drawn by the light and heat and by the sirens
    they stood in the street watching a house burn.
It was a small town; collectively, they were stunned
    at their own helplessness, and the sorrow of their neighbors,
An aging couple, who could rescue nothing from the fury—
    decades they had lived as friends, but now they stood apart,
Wondered at, even envied, as the chemistry of fire revealed
    how, from the start there was intention, the simplest gases
Reacting and catalyzing, impenetrable gravities dragging down
    the vacuum where worms commit wormholes,
Dark matter slowly filling with the nameless particles
    of a mass grave, the cavities of skulls,
In measures being kindled, in measures going out.

MULE

Down the street, by the line of crippled old men,
    each waiting his turn patiently to fill an urn
From the ruptured water pipe, a mule is dying,
    one of its legs shattered and gangrenous,
But still it walks, as if some labor remained for it
    among the piles of bricks and smoking timbers,
and one of the men strokes its flank as it passes,
    remembering the garden with perfect living rows,
His father's donkeys turning and turning the wooden wheel
    drawing from the shallow aquifer a stinking sulfurous water
That tasted of its own future seeping through communal graves.

GREEK FIRE

For the children of Sandy Hook, and all the others

The earth is made of stars, the teacher said.
    And: *All the stars are burning.*
We are learning how the stars are made:

A Big Bang, and it's day, the sad
    black holes bleeding dark all morning.
The earth is made of stars, the teacher said,

And we are made of earth. All the dead
    Lie in the earth, and we will too, returning,
Learning how the stars are made

To disappear: they are destroyed
    By light. They are brought to less than nothing.
The earth is made of stars, the teacher said,

And when they have bowed and entered
    It is from their own light they are hiding.
We are learning how the stars are made

And unmade. We betray them and we are betrayed
    By other Big Bangs, the fumbling of God.
The earth is made of stars, the teacher said,
    Unlearning how the stars are made.

II

URN

Drive your cart and your plow over the bones of the dead.

—WILLIAM BLAKE

We mercifully preserve their bones, and pisse not upon their ashes.

—SIR THOMAS BROWNE

RAINER MARIA RILKE, 1875–1926

There is a song the body sings to itself
    about time's arrow, that has pierced
Its sentimental shining heart: about the eternal
    flow of fire over the medulla oblongata,
And the oceanic backwash of lymph
    in the cells' interstices. Call that song an angel.
Call it space. The body sings, and does not know
    or care about the corrosive dark matter
Sealed in burial urns. The body sings, and when it stops
    for breath, nothing sings back its harmony.

LUIS OMAR SALINAS, 1937–2008

Over the Valle del Sol at midnight, one harrier hawk
    carries the flame of its singular heart, being
A hawk, being winged and alive, moonlight expanding
    its shadow dimly but vastly over a forest of saguaros
That surrounds the singular flame of a kangaroo mouse.
    A hawk takes no delight in the certainty of outcomes.
A hawk knows its hunger and carries it fiercely through the sky.
    But for the man who hears the hawk there is the contemplation
Of the image of endless hallways, each receding into darkness,
    each with a series of doors: behind each door an endless hallway.

MARY LOU WILLIAMS, 1910–1981

Death drives a Cadillac in the rock and roll metaphysic,
    and in the Appalachian canon owns a mountain railway.
If it *comes* you are transported. You're here, then you're there.
    Some say *pass away.* Some prefer *go back.*
If you *go* it's Dickinson's carriage. (*Could not stop. . . .*)
    In the new music, there will be no going anywhere.
If in the course of eternity everything averages out,
    you'll just stay put because really there is nowhere.
No measure. No line to separate the eighth note
    from the Steinway. A blank staff. No rest, but no accelerando.

LOUIS PORTERA, 1949–2009

At graveside they practice the prosody of passage. One must
    suppose a grave. They do their best to say what a life was
Made of. That was oceanic music like the last tide before a quantum
    Armageddon. Harmonics of the event horizon. Counterpoint
Of fistula. *Some find sepulchral vessels containing liquors, which time
    Hath incrassated into gellies.* They have put something in a hole
And covered it. That which is gone must be concealed. No: that
    which goes nowhere must be made invisible by an act of will.
There was music once, somewhere, and people danced. He remains there,
    incrassated to a conscious liquor in his own sepulchral vessel.

T. W. JACKSON, 1860–1957

Everywhere the earth is inoculated with bones. The boy can plow
    with a brace of mules at nine years old. At nine years old
He is *the man of the house*. Wind stalls over the sun-stroked prairie.
    Cotton saps all the virtue from soil within two generations,
And he is the third. His father is gone not *to* but *in* the war.
    Now the plow skews as the blade catches on the ribcage
Of a deer under four inches of dying topsoil. He was born on a vanished
    planet, but the bones of the deer remain, and his father's, and his own.
And still earth is dying of the plague we are, and craves the cure
    our bodies make, going down, going back, going in.

HERMES TRISMEGISTUS, DATES NONEXISTENT

Never-embodied one, the issue of death is altered for you,
    but it does not vanish, does it, for unvanishing, you persist
In the torqued minds of Rosicrucians, broke-back sorcerers, and students
    of the ahistorical Yeats: one knucklebone from your least
Finger would strike them blind. And yet I knew you, myth.
    You were that old woman on the stairs; you were that swarm
Of bees; you were that expression of everything that is the case.
    When you died, I alone heard the *pneuma* go out of you,
Not because I was wise or willing, but because I happened.
    Philosophers say: The world *worlds*. You should know. You are one.

THE GOOD COLLIE BUDDY, 1954–1971

The bones of the old dog settle under a pitch pine.
  Picked clean by buzzard and beetle, macerated by rain,
They shift but maintain essential form, sinking slowly
  Into topsoil, oblivious to the mattock and axe.
Time-lapse would reveal them disappearing into a muddy lake
  as the tree also vanishes and the underbrush rolls back
To admit the plow that will yank the skeleton up again.
  But the dog was a being of poised nerve and flame
That lingered awhile in the shadows, trembling, hungry,
  baffled, leaping darkward at the smallest motion from the edge.

MARTIN HEIDEGGER, 1889–1976

Perpetual noon. The sun stalls while armies march on the city.
    Somewhere, stuck in that absence, the old man sits down
At a plain wooden table. An assembly of statues watches him write.
    He who lives by the phenomenon will die of entropy.
Having signed his own death warrant, he lies down to wait.
    Stones from war engines batter the forum. Catapults arc in
The severed heads of spies and citizens. When do you stop being
    a philosopher? *Ancient frugality was so severe, that they allowed no gold*
To attend the corps, but only that which served to fasten their teeth.
    He is a mist now over the graveyard the enemy flattens.

MARY HELEN JACKSON HUMMER, 1885-1978

A tureen of soup steams on an embroidered tablecloth
    and the family gathers for the farewell dinner.
Grandmother sits in a chair in the corner. Yesterday
    he was born, a moment ago *he* played on the kitchen floor.
She understands the cliché of memory in the moment of letting go,
    but her intelligence fails her. It was not even yesterday.
Time is not a soup spoon, or even a hairball of tesseracted tangles.
    Steam has risen from stoneware bowls eternally.
She has always sat on this chair in her agony of loss.
    I is not even an other. *I* is an absence.

WALLACE STEVENS, 1879-1955

There was never a "first idea." There *was* a first mistake.
    The Opaline stone in this urne burnt upon the finger
Of the dead is what you see shining at the end of the mind.
    And the end of the mind is a brilliant place
Like a train yard in Michigan on a February morning in 1910
    where an endless row of coal cars shines black
Under the factory smokestacks. Your mind never went
    where the migrant worker lies in a boxcar's pile of straw.
Maybe he'll wake hungry there. Maybe he's dead. Who knows?
    His supreme fiction is what you call *an elixir, a pure power.*

HELENA BLAVATSKY, 1831–1891

We have placed the lamp in our basket, we are ready
    to journey beyond the end of time, but the ship
Is not here yet, it's late—again—and we protest
    to an official with a uniform and a gold pocket watch
Who cannot reassure us. The Himalayas stand before us,
    we travel there on the eagle of the soul,
But the body cannot follow, the train, we are told, is delayed
    forever, a bridge is down, armies are on the move.
Do you remember, my pure Beloved, how sunlight destroyed Odessa?
    This flesh is a vision of influenza, a shimmer of Bright's disease.

JUAN RAMÓN JIMÉNEZ, 1881–1958

You can follow The Beloved anywhere, through the next world
    to the market: there she buys mangoes and limes
And a rosary to replace the one the fascists stole. Light from the bay
    is like bleach on the memory of mass graves.
You sit at your desk naked in your muslin suit writing roses
    for the woman who has vanished. She may walk in
With heliconias in a vase—*this room is too dark and smells*
    of dust, like a tomb—and throw open the casement window.
One thing happens and then another, but which came after the other?
    A ticking in the ovaries and a world is born, or a cancer.

SAPPHO, 630(?)–570(?) BCE

What a surprise to be totally erased.
    All the flowers vanished; the naked urn
Lingered awhile, and then nobody can say
    what was left of it. Even of the poems
Only one stands complete. Fragments, bits of bone,
    dust. *I have a beautiful child, who looks*
Like golden flowers. A stone door opens and closes
    grinding dust beneath its massive lintel.
Absence waits patiently at the back of the queue of gods.
    Help me, as you helped them.

JULIUS ROBERT OPPENHEIMER, 1904–1967

This is the ark we build to deliver the dead
    to the realm of the dead. This is the sea
The ark sails on, silently, almost invisible in mist,
    the undated ruins of winds, floods, or earthquakes.
The wood of the ark is ancient, from the tree at the heart
    of the world, and the dead stand steady
On its well-joined decks. This is the map by which
    the Captain of the Dead navigates, gazing up at a dead
Sky crossed with dead constellations, worlds
    destroyed by nothing, going nowhere, sailing on.

FERNANDO PESSOA, 1888–1935

Many of us stood in the turnstile queue
    where the black train slid open its doors.
The arc of our line was the curve of our forgetting,
    polite but avid for completion. We were
Accidental in life as in the soul. One by one
    tokens dropped into the slot; one by one we passed
The threshold of the coach car, crossing into the golden
    gaslight, taking our seats—accidental, all our relations,
Though we acknowledged we shared one face. And *every atom*
    of me as good belongs to you, we wrote with our other mind.

MOSE, A TABBY, 1971–1986

He followed the Rat of Oblivion into a culvert pipe,
    for the smell of rat's blood was imperious
And impossible and wrong. The route ran deep
    and uncertain, but he could hear that furious
Scuttling. And he heard the cries of the upper world,
    birdlike, and windy, and human,
But he had to go where the black tail curled
    for his hatred of poisonous vermin,
Till he ripped that throat and drank that breath
    and slept on that fire-blasted hearth.

J., 920(?) BCE–(BIRTH DATE UNCERTAIN, DEATH DATE UNKNOWN)

If she ever lived at all—if any of us ever have, or do—
    if she ever breathed incense, or jasmine in the morning air,
If she ever drank ichor from the deep cold spring,
    if she ever twisted the neck of the dove,
Squeezed the blood from its breast on the dewy stone,
    plucked its body and gutted and roasted it
To nourish the priest who taught her to love
    the murderous godhead alone—
If she wrote down these words in a screed, my Lord,
    You'd exterminate nations to keep them whole.

WALTER WHITMAN, 1819–1892

Understand the need for so much loud machinery
    and enormous ugly buildings faced with unfathomable glass—
There can never be too much human desire, and never
    enough human dreaming. Destroy the world with your eloquence,
Children, and build it back again, and go to sleep
    proud you have been here and done things. But in your sleeping
Come quietly, leave behind the agita of your creation—
    where it waits for you in a compost of rose petals and slag,
You need trouble yourself to add nothing, nothing only.
    Only your nothingness, ours, is that lucky.

T. R. HUMMER, 1950 (ALT. BIRTH DATE 2011)–
DEATH DATE INSIGNIFICANT

I was born at the age of sixty, and I come into this new world
    with a bouquet of scars and old questions
From too long spent in the womb. You might as well be dead
    in there, where something thunders like a cartoon heart
On the other side of the wall—it's a clichéd quote
    from Poe, a motel room where nobody stays
More than an hour. Buried alive, I was more dead than you
    can imagine, and I rattled my chains in rhythm
To bad music on a radio. The afterlife should be otherwise,
    other and *wise* and *after.* Next time, timelessness.

LAURA NYRO, 1947–1997

Unfamiliar music is tiring: is that a melody,
    you find yourself wondering? Is that a chord?
Here everything is music, but inhuman. Nothing moves,
    and the long, deadening rhythm of it
Is stupefying. I am unpacking myself again and all
    I find is repetition. I am trying to feel at home.
I have arranged and rearranged the deep bass line
    my left hand wants, but the ground note
Echoes the slowest bolero. *And when I die*
    is a hook you can repeat until it passes.

CHARLES VERNON HUMMER, 1921–1994

Animals know how to die. To lie down in woods alone
    covered in cool mud from the creek bed, smelling
Alum and calcium in the fern bank; to rise, chasing
    a shadow into shadows, and realize you have left
Your body in that fierce, deadly joy, though you are still
    an animal. In the hospital there is a ticking of instruments,
The shimmer of surgical steel, a steady neon glow.
    How do we get from *here* to *here*? Where is that other world
That is nothing finally that we are not, where when we go
    we go nowhere that is not already human?

DAEDALUS, DATES UNKNOWN
OR NONEXISTENT

If everything that rises must have wings to lift it up,
    what is required to reach the underworld?
Some say a boat, but instead a magnificent machine
    presents itself to the mind: obsidian gears
Turn on lapis shafts, meshing with the energy
    of pure light focused through a crystal lens
In a golden housing set on cliffs above the sea
    where, at sunrise, its artifice will begin, and we
Will journey downward, as if our souls were made
    of wax and feathers, disintegrating for our fall.

EMILY DICKINSON, 1830–1886

No flies in the other life. No carriages. Called back,
    we travel without wings or wheels, trailing our bouquet.
It's a long stroll over the endless desert. And when the Great
    War overtakes us, we battle crinoline-to-hand,
Slashing a vanilla-scented heliotrope through legions
    of the already dead. Then the General reveals his flaming form
On the uttermost edge of Being. Dismounting his bone steed
    with a sweep of his hat, he bows—and seated
On his saddle we leave him there bemused, with a knot
    of blue field violets in one hand, in the other a lady's slipper.

CABEZA DA VACA, 1488/1490–1557/1559

Hell is what you make it, no matter what priests say,
    or how the chasms flame: earth was that way,
Earth was hell, and it was made hell by men.
    So now I have to do it all again:
On this side of the black river, horse and cannon,
    on that side infantry, and the quartermaster's wagons.
Armor does not serve us in this heat, but if we strip it
    off, who are we? Our labor in this pit
Is endless and empty and American. In the sulfurous
    quarries, men in hauberks labor, blind and furious.

ERATO, DATES UNIMAGINABLE

A hole in the ground containing the remains
    of an ancient cithara, kin to a guitar:
Neck warped, its ivory bridge grins
    like a mouth dithyrambed into a scar.
Bones too, of course, and a scattering
    of actual teeth: but how we love metaphor,
Here, at the poet's grave: the poet, a nattering
    cockroach of a human. We who inspired him are
Infinite, beautiful, cruel. Literally, he merely carried us
    Toward song. But as instrument, he was numinous.

SIR THOMAS BROWNE, 1605–1682

A peat-blacked urn on a workbench waits
    for the instrument of opening. Within:
Residues of a life, ritual's ideograms, all sediment.
    Here, a perfect peridot. There, shapeless gold,
A filling from a vanished tooth. Every fragment
    contains an unfathomable narrative called
Sir Thomas Browne that God stores in his infinite book
    and reads to the angels at bedtime
To frighten them to virtue. Human pain is an angel's
    nightmare. These urns contain that simple truth.

III

EON

I called my love.
She came, but not alone.
—RAINER MARIA RILKE

For Elizabeth, who gave me these poems.

To imagine you

To imagine you in my arms, I must imagine arms,
　　and to imagine arms I must have arms again.
And so the light breaks in, and the things of the world
　　assume their positions: tree here, stone there, sun
Just so in the sky. And the mountains tear themselves
　　out of the firmament, but gently and silently tear,
And the moon, old abused grandmother, watches over them.
　　You knew this already. You were there ahead of me,
Older soul of my soul. This world is yours. You give it
　　up, you give it back, and so embodied I imagine arms.

What world?

What world? I had been wiped clean. Fire
  ended it. Heraclitus raised an eyebrow,
And I was gone. The gasses of the afterlife
  absorbed the residues. Everything that I had been
Incised the cosmos like acetylene. And that was good—
  all the old errors reduced to vapor,
So that when you appeared the only thing
  I had to reckon with was coming back together:
I thought *Here needs rearranging,* and when you
  swept aside the pieces, I was home.

To wake again

To wake again in a bed, in a room with a window,
    with curtains trailing over a sill—I had forgotten
How simple it is. The eyes open and the body enters consciousness,
    the knowing that can be shared. A room with a chair and a mirror,
And in the mirror a wall with a photograph of a face
    I had seen in my dream. Seamlessly, the soul enters a room
Using a body for a doorway. And across the bed, still asleep
    Another body is dreaming of a face that might be photographed
Someday—unknowable unless you wake too, and see
    what soul is watching you sleep. I will dream all this in some future.

There is a house

There is a house on a great empty plain, under high empty hills
    and the air is turbulent with hawks circling over empty oaks,
And a bottomless lake whose troubled water is emptiness incarnate—
    a world so demanding to be filled that its blankness is a destiny
To anyone who enters: *here there be lacunae.* Opening the great front door
    we step into a river of fire that is only the wind of this place,
And are brought, you and I, to the center of its great need:
    Not ours, but given to us. Stay with me, beloved other: we are made
To break and break and break until the dust of us is forgotten
    and peace descends on the hills, the plain, the house, and we start again.

You spoke

You spoke your mind. You said *I have another mind:*
    A brace of oxen pulling a wagon down a rocky trail,
Axes breaking boles of smoke from the fiery pits of fields,
    an army of sowers scattering seed into the cinders
Where bits of armor rust, and the broken skulls of soldiers
    peacefully dissolve in the milkweed, two ravens negotiating
Over territory near a field mouse warren. You thought it
    grain by grain into its solitary order, in your other mind,
And every atom of it was alert to what might have seemed like dreaming
    except there were children in it too, releasing ships across a fountain.

What is a soul

What is a soul, said one child to the other while they dispatched
    their fleets across the fountain's uncertain water.
Just something grown-ups say when they don't know what they're saying,
    said the other, tossing in a stone, taking one ship under.
Is there really no such thing then? Who knows, said the other,
    watching a beetle flailing near the spot the ship foundered.
You were the child with questions; I was the child with no answers.
    We stood in the middle of each other's lives while the wind
Of the great world burned us, while the voice of the great world claimed us,
    while the soul of the great world sang to us, and we listened while we drowned.

Drowning

Drowning was a tedious journey. The wheels on the rails
　　made a sound like bees at labor. You put a drop
Of their honey on your tongue and we crossed a prairie.
　　When the train stopped we were nowhere. Even the train
Was gone. It was silent at the fountain's bottom. We found
　　ancient coins, gold, with our faces on them, and ivory
Intaglioed with our fingerprints. Everything subaqueous
　　resonated like a struck tuning fork. Then the conductor said
Next stop, pierced our tickets with a silver punch, led us
　　by our elbows to the platform of Terminal Earth.

Our earth

Our earth. It needs to be constantly imagined.
    It needs. And yet it is indifferent
To every human gesture. Already we have forgotten
    that we were children, and that we loved each other then
In spite of distances. The sun does not care
    what dark matter stood between; the desert hawk
Let eons pass before its claws descended.
    If I touch you now, no singularity.
The pillar of flame does not fall. And yet the ocean
    needs. The sky needs. And we are summoned.

A street corner

A street corner in Chicago. A street corner in Cairo.
    A street corner in Beirut. Dharamsala. San Francisco.
Called together by the great inaudible horn, by the klaxon
    on the bow of the ship of summoning, drawn
Together by the secret complementary spin
    of the atoms in our fingertips, we meet again,
You, my unknown soul—call it that—my interior
    other: numinous, yet in this light no more
Than who you are: a body meets my body
    everywhere in the earth's infinite inventory.

Flatwear

Flatwear meticulously packed in a kitchen drawer,
    a closet full of fresh-ironed shirts,
A spotless glass coffee pot, a blown-glass jar,
    sun angling through a glowing wall of glass brick.
A wheat field, grain arranged obsessively for the scythe,
    a fox's den where the kits line up for the teat,
A ray bent precisely where it breaks from air to water
    and on to the perfect lens of the perfect eye of a perfect fish.
You, in your brown shirt, on a flowered blanket by the ocean:
    the camera's iris opens, touched (as I am) by the light from your face.

You want to know

You want to know what is perfect in this—no, not *fallen*
    world: so much bad baggage in a simple phrase—
What is perfect in this *story,* because everything that is written
    is a world, and a world is everything that is the case—
So what is perfect in this *written world,* you wonder.
    But you have also written worlds; you already know
The answer: nothing, everything, anything you desire,
    there is nothing absolute here, no measure: so
How is this world not fallen? Because we won't let it be.
    The words fall from our bodies, and are our history.

Traffic

Traffic grinds in the avenue, flows through a mountain pass
    and stalls in a snowdrift, where the lost ones wonder
How long it will be before they give in to the Great Hunger.
    A cement truck stridors in the alley again—we've heard
That sound before. And farther off, a predictable train
    crashes its flatcars. But you are walking by the river
In your dream, where nothing repeats itself, not the sun,
    which is making its first setting, not the dog
At the end of its leash who has never smelled such miracles
    of tree and stone and water and self and human.

Tree and stone

Tree and stone and water and self and human:
    of which do we know least? one child demands.
This one is a sphinx. She is taller than the other child who stands
    behind her—the two are less than sisters, more than friends:
They are sphinxes, they have an answer, yet they want it back.
    The heroine hesitates. In the waiting air, a kite's beak clacks,
And she despairs of her good purpose. But now she speaks:
    Of tree, nothing; of stone and water, nothing. No mistakes,
One sphinx-child mutters. *Of self, nothing. Of human:*
    Less than nothing. Those words belong to us, the children said as one.

You, in your brown shirt

You, in your brown shirt, on a flowered blanket by the ocean:
    you ask for nothing, the light makes you feel very small
Under the usual sky, which, as usual, gives nothing anyway:
    the transaction *I ask, you give* is canceled here
Marked with the legend *merely human things*. You are the legend
    of human things, and as such you can ignore them
While an osprey loops high over the darkening water, asking,
    And a ewe wanders a low meadow out of sight of the osprey, asking,
And a fox leaps shadow to shadow in the copse where the sheep can't see,
    Asking, and I, invisible in a cloud of neutrinos, nonexistent, I am asking too.

The vocative O

The vocative O: O God of This Infinity, O my soul:
  I have compared thee, O my love, to a company of horses . . .
The perfect pure vowel will summons you *O fairest*
  among women, O ye daughters of Jerusalem, O my dove.
In the insurance office, on the factory floor, O: they stand and listen.
  Now is the time of the gathering. Now does the event horizon
Release its apocalyptic circle. Brilliant wind. Bright clouds close the horizon.
  On the killing floor the foreman pauses, the holy hammer hangs
Over the head of the chosen one. *O bull of Babylon.* My otherness: O hear
  The thunderous echo: *How beautiful are thy feet with shoes.*

Among ruins

Among ruins on a mountainside where the old world foundered,
    the children—two daughters—are playing while they wait.
One picks up the cornucopia of an ear and pretends to be hearing something:
    An ear listens to an ear, she whispers, laughing. The older other
Looks in a stone eye. *We're eye to eye now,* she is saying, but she sees
    herself in the granite torso shattered and peaceful in these weeds,
A lion's body, her own, with the smell of another age, another
    spirit, her *genius loci. These words are ours,* she starts to say,
But *No mistakes,* repeats her other mind. And finally she is human,
    one self among the trees, the wind, the crumbling stone.

What is a body?

What is a body? one of us said to the other.
    Ash, stone, blood in the water.
One said, *Is there no such thing then?*
    Certainly, came the answer,
Can you not feel my hand? It feels like wind
    the first voice said, *it feels like nothing at all.*
So there was nothing but nothing? Nothing ephemeral:
    Somewhere above us the mourners' feet
Rippled the grass and moved on. And when
    I kissed you, the dust on your lips was sweet.

The children are gouging

The children are gouging in the garden with small
    sharp shovels that shine like the royal toys
The emperor's heirs were playing with in columned halls
    when assassins did their deed of darkness.
They dig beside the gardenia bush—what if Mother finds them
    down in the place of the deep tap root, destroying
All she has grown? But they burrow their way to an old stone door
    that creaks its corroded hinges. They pull us up
From our earthen urn. They cut the winding cords. They slap us
    out of our absence: *our* children, the unborn.

Our earth. My hands

Our earth. My hands are black with it.
    When I touch your mind, your body is marked.
Summoned, we stand in the presence of our own skin
    and know what it belongs to. Long ago,
In a field surrounded by a forest, two seeds fell
    and tilth received them, and the small rain.
Then we were children. We had no names. We were
    simple expressions of our earth. It imagined us,
And was imagined by something nameless in return.
    Our need is an echo of its indifferent need.

The world we entered

The world we entered had purpose. In the diffuse light
    of the room where you sit reading, purpose enters;
In the bedroom where I cannot fall asleep, it comes right
    to the edge of consciousness. How can we love each other
Here, in the middle of brutal distances—but how can we not?
    Purpose enters, purpose with its steel shaft and shank,
Purpose with blood in its blood. I will not forget
    The dream in which the gazelle, at twilight, drank
From a fountain where ancient coins shimmered, and let
    the dark come down, with jackals gathered behind it.

You

You, that manifold syllable, denoting now another mind
    where my own mind once spun like a spider,
Denoting another, but also denoting myself, as in
    what are you doing, you fool, said in a vicious mutter
When nobody else is there—or *can you believe it*
    after a stroke of luck. And *you* in its plural form
Denotes us all. All destinations have secret
    journeys. *You* is a destination. *You in my arms*
Is a cosmos. You are traveling there through a wormhole,
    you, an ephemeron, a syllable, a soul.

Love that down the valley

Love that down the valley of the avenues comes flying through
    the "good buildings" of the Upper East Side—comes flying
Down Park Avenue by the Asia Society and turns past Hunter College
    to rendezvous with pigeons on Roosevelt Island: there is a home
Somewhere here with a warrior's name written on its threshold
    of stone, there is the Realtor of the Gods with a lease
And a dagger and a bowl of goat's blood, spilling: and love
    arrives like a hurricane blown through a subway tunnel,
Collecting the keys and sending a phalanx of doormen
    into that great or final darkness, gnashing and begging and wailing.

By the steaming river

By the steaming river, by the stinking waters,
    the jackals gather for reasons of their own devising.
Let the jackals be jackals. Buses and taxis sound
    another cry in the street's stream. You canter
Along the sidewalk, gazelle of my other being,
    to where the city opens out into another life.
Let the vultures go hungry, always. Let the shadows
    defend you. People eat lunch calmly in the bright cafés.
They are chattering of nothing. Let their music be your peace.
    Who says this world is not brilliance littered with bones?

In the dream that was no dream

In the dream that was no dream the fields were choked
    with urns, ash spilled from their cracked sides
And out of their broken mouths: ash and teeth
    and charred bits of bone buried the flax in airlessness.
That was one truth, an X without a referent, a simple problem
    without solution. And where then shall we turn?
Useless to petition the whirlwind, pointless
    to curse God and die when the world is dead already.
The swordless sword of heresy has already cut that knot.
    Lift up your eyes, the prophet says, fall asleep, try again.

To hold you

To hold you in my arms, I must stop imagining.
    The supreme fiction ends, and we look up
From the book, and there is the sun, an army
    of angels flying against its blindingness and vanishing.
In the borderland of the necessary illusion, a marker burns:
    Turn back. No, it is an angel with a sword of fire,
But the sword is the sun, and the angel throws himself on it.
    That much was easy enough, once I started walking
Toward the conclusion of vision, into my final life
    Where I stop imagining and hold you in my arms.

The most ordinary life

The most ordinary life, a glass of water, a potato
    bearing ideograms of earth onto the holy sideboard,
An open window. Over the threshold of nothingness
    we step onto a porch with chairs watched over
By a patient beagle. How simple that was. Do I remember
    a prophet wearing a sandwich sign bearing the legend
No way out of confusion? No, I remember nothing
    but nothing, and the creak of an opening door,
And eye-burning sunlight, and one step over the jamb,
    and you there as always, looking up and smiling.

CODA

The place feels right
since it's half dead to begin with.

—PHILIP LEVINE

CHEAP GLASS VASE AT THE JAZZ SINGER'S GRAVE

A black woman lies here, buried in a white grave.
    What do I do now, as snow gives way to pigeon scat
And rotting acorns even the squirrels will scorn?
    Everything whiteness concealed will boil to the surface
Under relentless light, the whole story of her life
    crushed between two dates. After that bracketed time,
Two men dug a hole, with a pickax first, then shovels.
    It was an April morning and a mockingbird swung its riff
From a live-oak tree. They stopped and ate potted meat
    on saltines from a greasy sack. One of them fell asleep
In the shade of a crooked marker. The other felt so alive
    he jitterbugged with his shovel on the edge of the raw pit
He was proud of making, singing her songs to himself: *Strange*
    Fruit. Black and Blue. When the mourners arrived
The gravediggers had disappeared. When the snowstorm hit,
    the mourners had graves of their own. Now the snow pays
Its respect by vanishing in turn, and here on the stone's footing
    A vase some lover of antique music bought
At Goodwill has outlived the cheap plastic flowers
    it was meant to hold forever. All it can contain
Is its own flaws. They distort the relentless sunlight
    so precisely that a bent ray burns a perfect blue note
Against the surface that holds her holy name. What do I do?
    Now that the snow gives way, I hum a little scat
Into the afternoon. *Ain't Nobody's Business If I Do.* There is Africa
    in my larynx, and Trinidad, there is Tibet, Spain,
And Detroit. Now that the light reveals me, I remember my own
    gravestone still crystallizing in a raw cliff beside a lake
Where one silent raptor glides, dancing over the water, hearing me sing.

    —In memoriam Philip Levine, 1928–2015

CPSIA information can be obtained
at www.ICGtesting.com
Printed in the USA
LVOW11s0839250318
571070LV00001B/72/P